HOW PARENTS CAN HELP STOP BULLYING

N C STELLA

UPFRONT PUBLISHING
PETERBOROUGH, ENGLAND

How Parents Can Help Stop Bullying?
Copyright © N C Stella 2007

ISBN 978-184426-411-7

First Published 2007 by
UPFRONT PUBLISHING LTD
Peterborough, England.

Printed by Lightning Source

i

Contents

PART TWO
HOW PARENTS CAN BE INVOLVED TO HELP
CHILDREN TO DEAL WITH BULLYING AND
PREVENTING THEIR CHILDREN FROM
BECOMING THE BULLY

Introduction

You are neither the first nor will you be the last parent to ask yourself, "What can I do to help my children with this bizarre world?"

As we see, hear and know, bullying is the major problem in our society. Its effects are even worse for our children and that's why it is important to understand how we can try to stop bullying.

Today's children are a troubled generation. Evidence of this is found in research of emotional and behavioural problems among children. And this is because children today live in a social world which has become poisonous to their development or a threat to their well-being and survival.

This book discusses how bullying can be the cause of children's distress and offers practical suggestions for both children and parents.

These are critical times and hard to deal with, especially for young people, but with a good knowledge or understanding about what bullying is and how it can be dealt with, both parents and children can successfully pass through this difficult time of modern life.

It is my pleasure, therefore, to provide this collection of practical information, which may help to answer the questions which bother many parents.

Chapter One
Understanding Bullying And How It Happens

What is bullying?

Bullying is the process of intimidating or mistreating somebody in a vulnerable situation. It is the wilful desire to cause pain or stress to another person. It can involve harassing, teasing, hitting and insulting others.

It is a behaviour, which can be defined as the repeated attack - physical or psychological, social or verbal - by those in a position of power, on those who are powerless to resist, with the intention of causing distress for their own gratification.

Bullying is also defined as a negative action through which someone intentionally inflicts, or attempts to inflict, injury or discomfort upon another. It can be carried out verbally, for instance by threatening, taunting, teasing and calling names. It can also be physical by hitting, pushing, kicking, pinching or restraining another. Also it is possible to carry out negative actions without the use of words or physical contact, by using expressions such as making faces or dirty gestures and intentionally excluding someone from a group.

Today, many youngsters are inclined to make insulting, hurtful remarks about fellow youngsters and others.

Recalls one of the students, "I was the shortest, smallest, and smartest kid in my class. Being the smartest kid and the shortest kid in the class was a disastrous combination - those who didn't want to hit me for being a runt, hit me for being a smart guy. In addition I was called so many abusive words; it was the hardest time of my life".

Harassing, teasing, stealing, spread rumours, damaging your belongings, calling names, threat and intimidation, making things up to get you into trouble and insulting others are the cruel pastimes of many young ones.

Children with physical handicaps, speech problems or obvious physical or behavioural peculiarities are a ready target for bullying by other children.

Also some bullying can be targeted because of the weight (too fat or too thin), if you are wearing spectacles or hearing aid, or if you are different colour or culture, etc.

Bullying is not an isolated event and it cannot be brushed off as a mere aberration. School bullying is a major problem in our society today. Many young people have committed suicide, become involved in drugs or dropped out of school at a very early age because of being bullied by their fellow students.

Most kids decide to take this kind of action because nobody has made an effort to help them understand what they're going through, and to help them deal with situations like this.

As bullying continues to hurt and affect some

children for long periods of time, they may try to defend themselves, which may cause more damage to one another. But many of them are defenceless when they face harassment, through not having the experience to be able to handle stress and anxiety in a positive way.

Even a single instance of more serious harassment can be regarded as bullying under certain circumstances; the definition given above emphasizes negative actions which are carried out repeatedly and over time.

Bullying can be carried out by a single individual or by a group. In the context of school the target has usually been a single person.

How to identify bullying

In order to identify bullying there must be an imbalance in strength, whereby the person who is exposed to the negative actions has difficulty defending him/herself and is somewhat helpless against the person who harasses.

The psychological effects of bullying can last in a person for a lifetime or affect future progress and even brain growth.

Bullying can have different meanings depending on where it takes place or who is involved.

In this book we look at bullying in schools and what effect it has on children. This will help parents understand what's going on in schools today and what can be done to make a better future for children before it's too late.

Chapter Two
The Causes Of Bullying

Bullying can be caused by so many things, for example changes in the family, changing views of discipline, the emotional attitude of parents, the use of physical punishment and violent emotional outbursts, being a victim of another bully, competition at school, poor childhood, the media, etc.

Changes in family

Many children suffer badly when there are changes within a family. For instance, when parents are divorced, most of the time children are the ones who are worst affected by the changes divorce may bring.

The divorce of one's parents can seem like the end of the world, a catastrophe that generates enough misery to last forever. It often triggers an onslaught of feelings of shame, anger, anxiety, fear of abandonment, guilt, depression, profound loss and even a desire to avenge. Watching the break-up of your parent's marriage can be one of the most painful experiences imaginable.

In general children who have recently experienced a family dissolution have a more difficult time with academic and social expectations at school than children from intact families or established single parent. Additionally, parents' divorce often affects the child's sense of emotional well-being and self esteem. And that's when some children become more aggressive, or violent.

Changing views of discipline

Changing views regarding parental discipline have also had an affect on today's children. Many parents seem to abdicate their authority. When this happens, children grow up with few, if any, rules or guidelines to regulate their behaviour.

In some cases, it seems like parents are reacting to the negative experiences they had in their own childhood. They want to be friends with their children, and not disciplinarians. "I was too lenient," admits one mother. "My parents were really strict; I wanted to be different with my child. But I came to realize I was wrong, and I wasn't fulfilling my responsibility as a parent." If parents are generally permissive and tolerant without setting clear limits, it can create aggressive behaviour in a child.

Emotional attitude of parents

The basic emotional attitude of the parents toward the child is very important, especially during his/her early years. A negative attitude, characterized by lack of warmth and involvement, clearly increases the risk that the child will later become aggressive and hostile toward others.

Use of physical punishment and violent emotional outbursts

When parents are using physical punishment on a child, or make emotional outbursts, like shouting or swearing, it can be very dangerous because it creates anger toward a child, and it can also increase the child's level of aggression.

The best way is to set clear limits and to impose certain rules on a child's behaviour, but it should not be done by the use of physical punishment or emotional outbursts.

Being a victim of a bully

It is very hard for some children to cope with bullying, especially those who have been bullied before. While some of the victims may become weak, isolated, depressed, insecure, etc, some victims can become very bad-tempered and want to avenge. The temperament of a child can play a big part in the development of an aggressive reaction pattern. A child with an active temperament is more likely to develop into an aggressive youngster than a child with a normal temper.

Competition at school

In some cases bullying is a consequence of competition for good marks at school. More specifically, it has been argued that the aggressive behaviour of the bully toward their peers could be explained as a reaction to frustrations and failures at school.

Poor childhood

Among the bullying or aggression-generating behaviour, poor childhood conditions in general, certain forms of child-rearing, and family problems in particular, are the main causes of aggression. It is natural to postulate that most bullies received a less satisfactory upbringing and experienced many family problems. A less satisfactory upbringing implies among other things that the child gets too little love, care and supervision, and that parents do not set clear limits to the child's behaviour. Family problems can include conflicts, failed inter-personal relationships between the parents, divorce, alcohol problems, etc.

Media

Most children who watch a lot of violence on TV, on video and in the movies often become more aggressive and have less empathy with victims of bullying. So to some extent, the media can also increase the level of bullying in our society.

In conclusion, as children grow up, it is very important that parents try to supervise their activities, monitor what they're doing and establish who are their friends. By doing this, the level of unwanted activities including bullying and anti-social, or criminal, behaviour could be reduced.

Chapter Three
The Effects Of Bullying

Bullying can cause so many effects including chronic stress which leads to health deterioration, involvement in crimes, suicide, involvement in drugs, promiscuous sex, etc.

Stress

When you feel stress, your heart rate and blood pressure soar, your level of blood sugar rises and hormones are released. And if stress becomes persistent, all parts of the body become chronically over-activated or under-activated. This may cause physical or psychological damage over time.

Of particular concern is the unhealthy way in which many children try to cope with stress. It is very depressing to find out that in their desire to escape from pain, children takes routes such as alcohol and drugs, truancy, delinquency, sexual promiscuity, aggression, violence and running away from home.

All these routes lead them into problems more overwhelming than those they were trying to escape; also those routes contribute to acts of violence.

Bullying can remove inhibitions and social restraints and can blur the way one interprets other people's action, making a violent response more likely.

Drug misuse and sexual abuse

Some of the children become involve in non-fatal crimes of violence or theft at school, some of the children drop out of school and involve themselves in drugs, some commit suicide because of not getting the help they need.

One youth recalls that some days, because of bullying by fellow classmates, he was so scared and unhappy that he couldn't concentrate on his studies through worrying about what other students would do to him.

And some of the children become involved in promiscuous sex at a very young age.

At the age of 14, Jane was regularly engaged in sex and was a heavy drug user. She was also a confirmed alcoholic and living an immoral life, but she admitted that she didn't like the life she was living nor the things she was doing.

Why then did she act as she did? Peer pressure!

"Everyone I was with was into these things, and that had a big effect on me," explains Jane, "and I didn't want to lose my friends".

"I was an emotional child," says John, a young man 20 years old. "At times I'm afraid and even intimidated by others of my own age. I suffer from depression, insecurity and, at times, I've even considered suicide."

Roselyn, 26 years old, describes herself as "emotionally very young", having "low self esteem". She adds, "I find it very difficult to lead a normal life."

John and Roselyn are reaping the consequences of a decision they made when they were quite young, to experiment with drugs.

Many youngsters today are doing likewise – injecting, swallowing, sniffing and smoking everything from cocaine to marijuana.

For some of them, doing drugs is a way to escape problems. Others get involved to satisfy their curiosity.

Others use drugs to ease depression, which was caused by being bullied. And once started, many continue using drugs for the sheer pleasure of it.

Considering youngsters, who use drugs to escape problems, like John and Roselyn, emotional growth comes from facing life's challenges, handling success, surviving failure. Youngsters who rely on a chemical refuge from problems hinder their emotional development. They fail to develop the skills needed for coping with problems.

Depression

Bullying can also cause depression whereby children who were previously docile become more confrontational, they also develop rebellious behaviour and even run away from home.

They become more isolated by withdrawing themselves from friends, or their friends withdraw from them, noticing an undesirable change in their attitude and behaviour.

They lose interest in almost all activities. Hobbies that were just recently considered intriguing are now perceived as boring. They develop sleeping problems by sleeping either too much or too little. They drop in academic performance by being reluctant to go to school at all. They develop feelings of worthlessness or inappropriate guilt by becoming highly self-critical, feeling like a complete failure, even though the facts may indicate otherwise.

For much of her life, one lady explains, she has struggled with negative feelings about herself. "Years of sexual abuse during my childhood killed a big part of my self-respect," she says. "I felt that I was completely useless."

James, too, looks back on his youth and says, "Deep within me there was a void and the belief that I wasn't worth much." The profound happiness that results from such feelings seems to be widespread today. One telephone counselling service for teenagers says that almost half of their callers express "persistent feelings of low self–value".

According to some experts, feelings of inadequacy emerge when people are made to feel worthless by others.

Such a state of mind may develop when one is subjected to constant berating, excessive and harsh criticism or abusive exploitation.

Whatever the reason, the consequences can be debilitating and even destructive.

Most people with negative feelings about themselves tend to distrust themselves and others, thus unwittingly sabotaging close relationships and friendships.

In a sense they create the very situations they fear most.

People who feel that way are often victims of their own disquieting thoughts.

They feel that they are never good enough. When something goes wrong, they instinctively blame themselves. Though others may praise them for their achievements, deep down inside they feel like a fraud that will be exposed sooner or later.

Believing that they are unworthy of happiness, many fall into self-destructive behaviour that they feel powerless to correct.

The victims of bullying are more anxious and insecure than other students in general.

Further, they are often cautious, sensitive, and quiet.

When attacked by other students they commonly react by crying and withdrawal.

Also they can suffer from low self-esteem, and they can develop a negative view of themselves and their situation. They often look upon themselves as failures and feel stupid and ashamed.

The victims can become lonely and abandoned at school, they do not have a single good friend in their class they can trust.

They are not aggressive or teasing in their behaviour. Also these children often have a negative attitude towards violence and the use of violent means.

They are more likely to become physical weaker.

Remember – the effects of bullying can last for a long time, often for many years, which is why it is important to decrease substantially the level of bullying among children. Most of the time a victim will often find him/herself in a difficult situation for a long time.

Further, the chances of the child being able to escape this situation are fairly small, unless special efforts are made to effect changes.

Part Two

*How parents can be involved
to help children to deal with
bullying and preventing their
children becoming the bully*

Chapter Four
What Can Be Done To Stop Bullying?

The most important thing that can help to reduce the number of bullying cases in our society is to involve parents in educating children about dealing with different issues in life. I believe home is the first school of everything and parents have to play the main role in teaching and educating their children.

Although we have schools, it is the parents' job to build a strong foundation that can lead children in a better way, when they start school.

If a child has a better foundation, it makes him/her even stronger to deal with different situations in a wise manner.

It might seem very hard to take this responsibility, especially in this busy and hectic world where most parents work hard and long hours and leave children unsupervised for lengthy periods of time.

No matter how little time we have with our children we must make the most of it, regardless of how tired we may be. Parents cannot rely on schools to do all the teaching because it's not enough.

Today, because many family members are busy and always on the move, they find it difficult to meet together. Eating has become a haphazard, do-your-own-thing affair in many households.

Besides filling a physical need, enjoying a meal together as a family can satisfy even more important needs such as warm communication and family bonding.

Explains one mother, "Although I work, with my children going to school, we normally organise our schedule so that we can have one meal together.

During mealtimes all of us feel free to talk about the day's events and to share our problems, thoughts, plans, likes and dislikes.

"Without a doubt mealtimes draw us closer together."

Adds another parent, "Preparing meals with my daughters gives us opportunities for intimate communication.

"The girls enjoy doing things together in the kitchen and at the same time they are learning valuable skills.

"Thus, we are able to combine work with pleasure."

Some families eat together and use this time for talking about different issues they faced in different places.

Everyone enjoys a fine meal. Add to the meal good conversation and warm association with people you love, and it becomes a delightful event that satisfies more than just a hunger.

Families must make a practice of gathering together at least once a day to share a meal.

Mealtime gives the family the opportunity to discuss the day's events or plans.

Parents who listen to their children's comments and expressions get a glimpse of the thinking and feelings of their children.

Over time, the happy, relaxed association enjoyed at

mealtime builds a sense of security, trust and love within a family that adds stability and unity.

Other families have the habit of turning on the TV during the meal, effectively robbing themselves of any meaningful communication.

In addition to communication, children need reasonable boundaries.

A lack of clear limits can be at the root of juvenile delinquency.

If a child is endlessly indulged and never hears the word "no" or experiences limits, he/she never has a chance to learn that other people have lives, emotions, needs and wills of their own. Without a well-developed sense of empathy, the child will not be able to love.

Some parents believe that children should be free spirits and that to impose obligations or requirements would place an unfair burden on their offspring and deprive them of their childhood.

However, their failure to set limits may have disastrous results. They don't realize that children who receive little discipline may find it difficult to become self-disciplined.

However, parents are always alert to opportunities to build their children.

If parents are very busy, one of the best opportunities to communicate with their children is during the meal when they are sitting in the house; it can be lunch, supper or dinner.

Regularly sitting down together for a meal offers parents a unique chance to build a deeper love within their children. By cultivating a happy and relaxed atmosphere, you can make mealtimes an enjoyable and uplifting experience for your children too.

This is one way to get closer to the children, even if you seem to be occupied with the world's tasks.

Parents are the primary protectors for each child's health, education, intellect, personality, character and emotional stability.

Parents can better give their children wise direction if they understand their feelings and circumstances. Encourage good communication with your child, as children who are encouraged to talk out their stresses will be less prone to act them out through misconduct.

A strong emotional connection to a parent is the best guarantee of a child's health and the strongest barrier to high-risk behaviour.

Being a responsible parent thus means that you make sure that your children's needs are satisfied, including their need for all necessary forms of education and close friendship with their parents.

It means helping children to become capable, respectful and honest adults who treat their fellow man with kindness and respect.

As parents we have the privilege of helping our children to choose friends wisely. However, there's a problem. Many children feel closer to their fellow youngsters than to their parents and this is because many parents doubt their own moral authority.

Parents must shoulder the responsibility to reach out to, and stay involved with, their children.

Parents need to know that children will look to their friends if they're not getting what they need at home.

The key is to be close to the children, and that's when opportunities to talk will come naturally.

Explains one father, "My son and I worked together on household projects, we took trips together, and as a result, my son always felt that he could express himself freely."

Chapter Five
Guide Your Children In A Wise Way

Obedience and respect

In order to guide their children safely, parents have the responsibility to teach them the importance of honouring their parents. Honour involves recognizing and respecting constituted authority.

Showing honour means more than just rendering formal respect or begrudging obedience. It also means considering someone as of great value.

Parents should thus be viewed as precious, highly esteemed and dear to children. This involves having warm, appreciative feelings for them.

Developing personal defensive values

Every parent must fight against bad thinking, values and the peer pressure. In order to resist this daily attack in our mind and hearts we need to develop defences.

Such defences are especially necessary for our children, since they are not born with defences that can counter the challenges of the world. As children grow up, it is vital for parents to help them to develop their own defences.

Helping children in searching for friends who will build them in a good way, and not destroying them.

Understandably children like the company of other children, but exclusive companionship with other inexperienced ones will not promote the wisdom and confidence a parent wishes for the child. Look at the example below:

A mother said, "I have one fine daughter, but I admit that training her hasn't always been easy."

"In the area where we live there are few young ones of her age well-mannered enough to associate with her. However she had one friend from school that was an outgoing and cheerful young lady. Her parents were more liberal than we were. She was allowed to stay out later than our daughter, wear shorter skirts and watch un-suitable movies. For a long time our daughter had difficulty in seeing our point of view. To her, her friend's parents seemed more understanding, whereas we came across as being too strict. Only when her friend got in trouble did our daughter realize that our firmness had served to protect her. We are very glad we didn't weaken in our stand for what we believed was right for our daughter."

Many children have learned the wisdom of seeking their parents' guidance in this matter of association. Also it helps them to distinguish between right and wrong especially when it comes to decision making.

Helping them to deal with the pressure to conform

Closely related to association is peer pressure. Day after day, the pressure to conform attacks our children's defences.

Since children usually seek the approval of those in their own age group, peer pressure can squeeze them into the mould that the world views as desirable.

Help children to think and differentiate wisely

Explains one parent, "My daughter always wants to wear what other youngsters are wearing, so we patiently reasoned with her on the advantages and disadvantages of each request.

Even with fashion that we judged unobjectionable, we followed the counsel we heard a long time ago, 'It is a wise person who is not the first to adopt a new fashion nor the last to leave it.'

Another parent countered her children's peer pressure in another way. She recalled, "I took an interest in my children's interests and regularly went to their room to talk to them. These long conversations enabled me to shape their ideas and help them to consider other ways of looking at matters."

Peer pressure will not go away, so parents are likely to face a constant struggle to reason and help their children bring their thoughts under control, in obedience to their parents.

Helping them to understand and explaining the powerful attraction of entertainment

A third influence that parents may find it hard to deal with is entertainment.

Naturally, young children love entertainment. Many older children also eagerly seek amusement. But if satisfied in an unwise way, this desire can break down their defences. The danger mainly comes in two forms.

First, much entertainment reflects the world's debased moral standards, yet it is invariably presented in an exciting and attractive way. This poses a real danger for young ones, who may not perceive the pitfalls.

Secondly, the amount of time spent on entertainment can also cause problems. For some youngsters, having fun becomes the most important thing in life, absorbing far too much time and energy. As the saying goes, "The eating of too much honey is not good." Likewise, too much entertainment can dull the appetite for physical sustenance and lead to mental laziness.

How have parents coped with this challenge?

One parent, a father of two, explains, "We wanted our children to have wholesome recreation and enjoy themselves, so we regularly went out as a family and they also spent time with friends both at home and out of our home. But we kept recreation in its place.

"They learned to become workers at home and at school. We also made a habit of dedicating weekends as family days. We would go swimming in the afternoon and have a special meal in the evening".

The comment made by this parent shows the value of balance in providing wholesome entertainment and in assigning it to its proper place.

Help them to trust in you this will help develop personal defences. As a parent, you will have to go on bringing them up with discipline. Mental regulation means helping children to view things. You can accomplish this by having regular family religion studies or family discussion on different issues we read and hear on the news every day and get each other's views.

This can uncover the children's eyes so that they may see the wonderful things in the universe.

Remember - once a child has learned to respect and honour you as a parent and look at you as a precious mother or father, they will develop a sense of appreciating others and have respect to others and their ways. This will help a child not to bully others and will also develop personal defences and capabilities to be able to deal with being bullied by others and be able to make wise choices and decisions.

Chapter Six
Communicate With Your Children

C hildren today are growing up in a world that can at times seem frightening. Some of them watch helplessly as their parents separate or divorce. Others see their schoolmates succumb to the perils of drugs and crime. Many face pressure from peers of both genders to get involved with sex.

Children need a firm moral centre if they are to cope with challenges that face them.

They need the kind of anchoring that helps them pick appropriate friends, make the right decisions and view others empathetically.

Parents needs ongoing communication with their children and hence help their children to avoid bullying by encouraging them to watch their association, walk away from fights and talk to their parents.

Watch their association

Often children find themselves in the middle of a fight because they associate with the wrong crowd. Of course, giving a cold shoulder to their schoolmates could alienate them or make them hostile toward their schoolmates.

If they are friendly and polite to them, they may be

more inclined to leave them alone.

Encourage your child to walk away from fights

Avoid forcing one another to fight. Even if you come off the winner in a fight, your opponent may simply bide his or her time for a rematch.

So firstly, try talking your way out of a fight. If talking doesn't work, walk - or even run - away from a violent or confrontation.

And remember, a live dog is better off than a dead lion. As a last resort, take whatever reasonable means are necessary to protect and defend yourself.

Encourage your child to communicate with you

Children do not very often report their school problems to their parents, for fear that their parents will see them as cowardly and chide them for not standing up to the bullies. Often, though, parental intervention is the only way to stop the trouble.

All parents make mistakes and may regret the way that they handle certain situations.

Nevertheless, parents should keep trying not to give up doing what is right for their children.

Parents may feel like giving up, especially when they sometimes just can't understand their children.

It would be easy to conclude that the younger generation is different and difficult.

But really children today have the same weaknesses that earlier generations had, and they face similar temptations, although the pressure to transgress may have increased. The only difference now is that we have new technology; so many things has been modernised and updated.

Therefore, one parent, after correcting her children, softened her words by kindly adding, "Your heart only wants to do what my heart wanted to do when I was your age."

Parents might not know much about computers, but they know all about the learning of the imperfect flesh.

Perhaps some children express little enthusiasm for their parents' guidance and even rebel against the discipline they receive.

Once again, however, endurance is essential.

Despite initial reluctance or periods of defiance, many children eventually respond.

Explains one man, "When I was a teenager, I felt that my parents' restrictions were unfair.

"After all, I reasoned, if my friends' parents permitted something, why couldn't my parents?

"And I got really annoyed when they, at times, punished me by not allow me to go canoeing - something I loved. Looking back, however, I realize that the discipline my parents gave me was both effective and necessary.

"I am grateful that they gave me the guidance I needed when I needed it."

There's no doubt about it. Although our children may sometimes have to be in an unhealthy environment, they can still grow up to be fine adults.

When wisdom enters into your heart and knowledge itself becomes pleasant to your very soul, thinking ability itself will keep guard over you, discernment itself will safeguard you, to deliver you from the bad ways.

Carrying a child in the womb for nine months is not

an easy task. And the following 25 years may bring their share of pain along with happiness.

But because parents love their children very much, they must be ready to strive with all their might to protect them.

No greater cause for thankfulness do the parents have than these things that they should be hearing, that their children go on walking safely.

Chapter Seven
Understanding Your Child's Present Environment

D o you consider your children to be an inheritance of great value? Or do you view them as a financial burden with no guarantee of success?

Rather than bringing monetary profit, raising children costs money until they can sustain themselves. Just as managing an inherited fortune requires good planning, so does successful parenting.

Caring parents want to give their children a good foundation in life. Although bad and very sad things may happen in this world, parents can do much to protect their children.

Instead of letting children to take control of any kind of situation, parents should show genuine interest in what is going on in school and home.

Explains one girl, "I appreciated very much the practical suggestions my parents gave me when I needed help, and I felt that they cared for me and were supporting me.

As parents, they were quite firm, but I knew that they were my real friends.

Even when I was so upset over my schoolwork that I was depressed and had a problem sleeping, my parents also spent considerable time talking with me, and helping to recover mental balance."

Considering the challenge that parents face in protecting their children today, because of a decline in the quality of family life and an increase in poverty, the number of children who live on the streets is increasing in many countries. Child labour is the result of a failure to protect youngsters from exploitation.

Drug abuse also destroys many young ones.

For example, when a certain teenager became a drug addict, peace disappeared from his home.

Besides the emotional strain experienced by his parents, there was the struggle to finance his recovery and pitiless narcotics dealers came to their door demanding payment.

Despite the pressure of life, however, many parents continue the struggle of providing their children not only with food, clothing and shelter but also with protection from violence, drug abuse and other problems.

This is a noble endeavour, but is it enough?

What about protection from emotional harm?

Many realize that successful parenting includes the tackling of challenges that involve their children's choice of friends and recreation.

How can parents seek to protect their children and prepare them for good adult life?

From the time that children are infants, most loving parents always involve them in their daily activities. Instead of just socializing with their adult friends, parents have their children wherever they go, and guide them properly.

Parents must teach their children to take care of home, to be economical, and to take care of their belongings, like clothes etc.

Parents should help them to choose a profession and to reconcile their responsibilities with spiritual interests.

How vital it is to get to know your children and provide parental guidance! Let us examine three areas in which parents might do this:

(1) Prepare your children to cope with emotional stress in school. Emotions are powerful, they can affect the way you think and act. They can motivate you both for good and bad at times. They may even seem to overwhelm you. A part of being a responsible parent, however, is teaching your children to control their emotions.

As young people, they are also inexperienced so as they encounter new situations and challenges for the first time, it is only natural to feel insecure and perhaps overwhelmed.

Parents should help them to understand that the key to control their emotions is learning to control their thoughts, because negative thoughts can sap them of the energy they need to take action.

But how can they learn to think positively and thus be helped to control their emotions?

One way is to refuse to dwell on negative things that make them feel depressed or insecure.

They can also focus on things, which are serious and righteous. They can replace negative thoughts with positive ones.

Although it may seem a bit difficult, with effort it can be done.

It may well be that they feel insecure when they are confronted with a new or unfamiliar task.

But they can control such feelings of insecurity by

refusing to dwell on negative thoughts.

Let them focus on learning to do the task competently, ask questions, and follow instructions.

The more competent at tasks they become, the less insecure they will feel.

Don't let them dwell on their weaknesses, which can prevent them from making improvements.

Another way, which can help them to control their emotions, is to set modest, realistic goals and accept their limitations.

Also avoid unfair comparisons with others. Let each one prove what his/her own work is, and then they will have cause for exultation in regard to him/herself, and not in comparison with other people.

Managing anger can be another difficult challenge.

Parents should help their children to control their thoughts, so that they won't end up in trouble.

For example, when someone upsets them, let them try to understand why that person behaved that way.

Was that person deliberately trying to hurt or cause pain? Could it be that he/she was acting impulsively or out of ignorance?

Making allowances for the mistakes of others can help to slow down the feeling of anger.

If necessary, discuss the matter with the individual, or perhaps the best thing to do is simply to let the matter drop, let go of the anger and move on with life.

Interestingly, some friends can have an influence on how children deal with anger; so don't let them be friendly with anyone given to anger, and with anyone with negative thoughts or involved in bad things/activities, so that they may not get involved with his/her path.

Also as a parent, you can help your children overcome any negative attitude by encouraging, build up, and motivate them to participate in different activities, which may result in developing new skills.

Consider Christopher, a 14-year-old boy.

Besides internal turmoil as a result of bodily changes, he experienced emotional stress because of parental disunity and lack of attention. What can be done for young people like him?

Although it is impossible to shelter your children from all anxieties and bad influences, never give up your role as a parent. Without being overprotective, discipline your children with understanding; always remember that each child is unique.

By showing kindness and love, you can do much to make a young person feel secure. This will also prevent him/her from growing up lacking confidence and self-respect.

Regardless of how successful your own parents were in satisfying your emotional needs, a few things can assist you to succeed as a truly helpful parent:

- Avoid being so absorbed in your own difficulties that you ignore the seemingly small problems of your children.

- Endeavour to have pleasant and meaningful daily communication with your children.

- Promote a positive attitude regarding how to solve problems and deal with people.

Looking back on her years as a young girl, Jane recalls, "I had to learn that you cannot change people to be what you want them to be. My mother reasoned with me that if I saw something in others that I didn't like, what I could do was avoid being like them. She also said that the best time to change my own ways would be while I was still young."

(2) Show them how to satisfy their spiritual needs.

Children benefit a lot when parents set a good example in showing faith in God or whatever good thing they believe in.

In order to seek divine guidance, you must acknowledge your own spiritual needs.

Despite all the hard work involved in providing guidance, emotional support and spiritual help, parenting can be rewarding.

One parent comments: "I cannot even imagine not having my children. There is so much good that we can share with them."

In explaining why the children are doing well, the mother adds: "We are always together, and we try to make things festive and happy. And, most importantly, we always pray for the children."

Parents should schedule time with their children so they can read God's word; considering His principles in a positive atmosphere can help your children to be confident and to have real hope for the future.

(3) Help your children to choose an appropriate type of secular work.

Since a person's secular work not only affects his financial situation but also takes much of his time, good parenting includes considering each child's interests and abilities. Since no conscientious individual wants to be a burden to others, parents should think seriously about how their children can be prepared to sustain themselves and the family.

Would your children need to learn a trade in order to make a decent living?

As a truly caring parent, make consistent efforts to help your children develop such qualities as a desire to work industriously, a willingness to learn and the ability to get along well with others.

Explains one lady, "My parents had me working for them in their business. They suggested that I give a percentage of my earnings towards our household expenses and keep what was left for my own spending and savings. This gave me a heightened sense of responsibility that proved very useful later in life."

Chapter Eight
How To Help Bullied Children Cope With The Situation

A bullied victim needs help. But they can't get help on their own, until a parent or an adult has recognized the problem and take it seriously.

As the victim is usually a child who is anxious, insecure, with low self-confidence and with no friends, it makes the situation even harder to be solved. This is because in most cases the victim of bullying remains silent, fearful of making the situation worse and being hurt more - both physically and emotionally - not being believed, being seeing as a trouble maker, being blamed for provoking it, being ostracised by other students and getting the bully into trouble.

When they need closeness, and assurance in order for them to be open and be able to explain what has happened, it is important for parents to try to help the victim become better adjusted, quite independently of any current bullying situation.

If your child has been bullied, do not be ashamed of the situation.

The fact is bullying can overtake the finest of young people.

Indeed, the research shows that painful emotions

have afflicted some who strove their best to do what is right and stay out of trouble, regardless of their age.

As with any other skill, the ability to cope requires practice. Watch a skilled football player, he is able to use his head and feet in ways that are nothing short of amazing. Yet, how did this player develop such skill? Through years of practice, he learned to kick the ball, run with it, feint, and so on, until he became proficient at the game.

Therefore, parents need to help and encourage the victim in developing coping skills, by practicing, and encourage their children to communicate, no matter how bad the situation. Without good communication, the problem gets even harder to be solved, because no one knows what's going on.

Explains one girl; "I'd just started at secondary school when my baby brother was born. He was born with a disability and also had brain damage. My parents had to keep going to the hospital for his appointments. I'd often go along to support my parents so I missed school sometimes.

"That's when I started to get bullied. A group of girls started shouting things at me when I did go in, saying I was fat and ugly, and that I was lying about my little brother's illness to get attention. Before long, they were turning people against me and getting everyone to ignore me. Then I started to get horrible phone calls. I dreaded the phone ringing and hated going to school. I felt lonely and worthless.

"I kept crying at home and snapping at my parents and my sisters. I knew I was being horrible, but I just felt so unhappy and angry.

"Why are you being like this? asked mum, but I

couldn't tell her.

After a year, though, I started to put my feelings down on paper.

"Whenever I walked into school my nightmares started and I decided to write them down on the paper.

"I hid my letter under my pillow. A few days later, I got home from school and found mum in tears, holding my letter.

"What's going on? She asked. I started to cry, and decide to tell her everything.

"Telling mum what was going on made me feel better.

"But she had so much on her mind, with my ill baby brother, and I think at first she thought my problems might be sorted at some point.

"'They're probably jealous,' she said. 'They'll get bored and stop soon.'

"But they didn't stop. I stopped eating, and I didn't even feel hungry.

"Within just a few months I'd lost two stone. My parents went to see my teachers.

"By then I'd started refusing to go at school at all, too scared of what might happen.

"So my parents had to find me another school, where I started at spring time. Although I left, my bullies kept on sending me threatening messages, but I decided to stop reading them, and then I decided to change my phone number.

"It took me a while to get my confidence back.

"But now I love my new school, and I'm so grateful to be there.

"And because I'm happier, I'm being nicer at home.

"And that was when I realized how important it is to

open up your worries and troubles to your parents, so those problems can be sorted out."

Nevertheless, bullying in a child can exact a heavy toll on parents.

"Walk an emotional tightrope," says the mother of one bullied child." I'm concerned, scared, hostile, angry and exhausted."

Another parent admits, "I would go out and see a mother shopping with her daughter, and my heart would break because I felt I had lost that connection with my own daughter, and I would never have it again."

Such feelings are normal. At times, though, they may become overwhelming.

If that happens, why not confide in a trusted friend? A true companion loves you all the time, and is a friend that is born for when there's distress.

Never get discouraged or blame yourself

Many parents of bullied children become intensely discouraged and feel that they are somehow to blame for the situation.

"When your child is bullied," admits one parent, "you feel guilty and no one can tell you any different. You keep wondering, 'Where did we go wrong? Where was the turning point? How did we contribute to this?' etc."

Parents should keep their thinking balanced in this regard, and they shouldn't be too hasty to blame themselves or their children who are victims. The important thing is to provide support for the victims.

If the victim is plagued with feelings of low self-worth, parents can certainly help by not making judgemental statements like, "you shouldn't feel that way" or "that's the wrong attitude to have".

Instead, strive to be empathetic by showing similar feelings.

Remember, a person who is genuinely bullied really hurts; the pain is not imagined, nor is it feigned simply to elicit attention.

After listening, try to draw out the victim, ask why he/she feels that way.

Then gently and patiently help the victim to see why such a low assessment of him/herself is not warranted. Reassurance of God's love and mercy may help to alleviate the victim's anxieties.

Get the victim involved with extra activities

There may be further practical steps you can take. For instance, you may need to make sure that the victim is getting a proper amount of rest, nutrition and exercise.

It is also desirable, if there's a hint of interest, that the victim can undertake some kind of physical training, or engage themselves in some suitable sport, which can result in a better physical coordination and less body anxiety, which will increase their self confidence.

Taking part in sports or activities for which the victim has a certain talent will probably help them to get in contact with peers they haven't met before.

A new environment can be quite important, as the victim will not be evaluated here on the negative conceptions of his/her value that many classmates may have.

And in order to improve the victim situation at school, parents can actively encourage the victim to make contact with some calm and friendly student in the class, who has so much in common.

For example, she/he can make contact with children who have similar interests or a similar personality.

If parents discover that their child is bullied, most of them tend to increase their efforts to benefit the child and protect him/her from disappointment.

Although this is meant only to benefit the child, it may have negative consequences in the long run.

An overprotective attitude on the part of the parents can increase the child's isolation from peers, and create attachments to the adult word, which actually inhibits the process of establishing contacts with peers.

Against this background it is important for the parents consistently to support the child's possible tendencies toward engaging in contacts and activities outside the family.

At the same time parents should try to follow up their children's daily routine/activities, in order to know what going on in their children's life, and offer some support where necessary.

Admittedly, bullying in a child can be a harrowing experience, for the victim and for the rest of the family.

Remember - in the end, patience, perseverance and love will provide a foundation for helping a victim of bullying. And also in order to decrease the risk that an anxious and insecure child will develop into a victim, it is important that parents try to help their children towards greater independence, greater self-confidence and the ability to assert themselves among their peers.

Chapter Nine
Dealing With The Bully

As we know, bullying behaviour is demeaning and frightening. Allowing bullying to go unchallenged does not provide children with a safe and educationally stimulating learning environment. And if this behaviour is not stopped, the bully will end up in a very bad way.

If parents know, or suspect, that their child is bullying other children in school or at home, it is very important to take action immediately.

The aim of dealing with the bully is simply to make him/her stop that negative attitude.

When talking to a bully, parents must make it clear that they take bullying seriously and that they will not tolerate any such behaviour in the future, and so it must stop.

It is the parents' responsibility to clear up bullying problems; parents can do a great deal to improve the situation.

As has been described, children who are aggressive have a high risk of later engaging in anti-social behaviour such as crime, drugs and alcohol abuse.

It is therefore important to try to help bullies to change their negative attitude and behaviour toward others.

In many cases, aggressive children often have problems conforming to rules and their family relationship is neither very good nor organized.

Therefore, it is important that the parents work together with the child to try to agree on a few simple family rules.

These rules should be written down and put in an open place in the house.

It is important that parents give the child much praise and appreciation when he/she follows the rules agreed.

It is easier for a child to change her/his aggressive behaviour, if she/he feels liked, appreciated and loved to some extent.

However, if the child breaks the agreed rules, it is essential that he/she will take responsibility for doing so, and therefore he/she must be given some form of discipline.

Before bringing the matter up, parents must consider what kind of disciplinary action might be appropriate.

The disciplinary action should be associated with some degree of discomfort or unpleasantness, but not a punishment inflicted on the body.

Parents should also need to teach their children how to discern right from wrong, not by irritating them but by bring them up tenderly with good training and advice.

Emphasis on moral instruction is lacking in many homes today.

Some believe that, "at some point children should decide for themselves what values to accept".

Does that make sense to you?

Just as young bodies need proper nourishment to grow up strong and healthy, so young minds and hearts need instruction.

If your children do not learn moral values from you

at home, they are likely to adopt the views of their schoolmates and teachers or those of the mass media.

Also, parents need to be reasonable. While parents give their children all help they can, they shouldn't control their every action. Although sometimes children can take you to the point where your patience wears thin, it is easy to get angry or demanding and this can cause frustration for the children.

Parents need to look for opportunities for their children to do things with others under circumstances that they approved.

So they would approach them and say, 'Did you know that so-and-so is doing this and that? Why don't you go too?'

Or if the kids asked us to take them somewhere, we pushed ourselves to go even if we were tired, just to avoid being un-reasonable.

Therefore parents need to be fair, considerate and yielding towards children.

Most bullying occurs when adults are not around or do not know what the children are doing.

Accordingly, it is important for the parents to try to get to know who their child's friends are, and what they usually like to do.

A good way of finding out more about this is to spend time together with the child and his/her friends.

Being together with a child also provides opportunities for common positive experiences, and for a better understanding of a child's personality and reactions.

In this way, a more trusting relationship may develop, which can make a child more inclined to listen to and be influenced by the parents.

The parents may then also be able to help their child find less aggressive - and more appropriate - reaction patterns, perhaps by involving them in activities that develop physical strength or some special talents.

Chapter Ten
House Rules And Their Importance

House rules are the evidence of parents' love and concern towards their children. Therefore every house needs to have rules and follow them.

If we bring up children under rules we set, from the early age, there will be family stability, there will be security whereby children will feel safer, there will be affirmation and acceptance in the family, parents and children will spend more time together, children will learn to value things and communicate well and also they will be able to take responsibility for the future.

One day you may think differently about a home without rules.

Consider a study involving young women who grew up with few house rules and little or no parental supervision.

Looking back, none of them viewed the absence of discipline positively. Instead, they saw it as evidence of their parents' lack of concern or capability.

Understandably, children may long for a life away from their parents' authority.

But would they really be better off without parents' restrictions?

You probably know youngsters who can stay out as late as they want, can wear anything they like and can go with their friends whenever and wherever it suits them.

Perhaps the parents are simply too busy to notice what their children are doing.

In any case, this approach to child rearing has not proved successful.

The lack of love you see in the world today is largely due to it being filled with self-raised people, many of whom grew up in homes without restraint.

Therefore, in order to help build a strong bond with our children, we must make sure we start by providing them with a clear guidance of what is acceptable and what isn't acceptable in society.

And also we must make clear the consequences of disobeying the rules.

We must teach them the advantages of being obedient, whereby more will be given to obedient children as long as they will take seriously whatever tasks their parents assign them.

We must also teach them to take the initiative, for example, encourage them to pursue various initiatives, like offering to wash the dishes, sweep the floor, make the grocery list or tidy up their rooms if you haven't assigned any task to them.

Also parents must encourage the children to take responsibility for their own actions. For example, if children disobeyed or broke the rules, first encourage them to speak the truth, tell them to be honest and specific about details.

Explain to them tall-tales may undermine any remaining trust parents may have in them, but avoid justifying or minimizing what happened.

Always remember that, "an answer, when mild, turns away rage."

Encourage your children to apologize, expressing regret over the worry, disappointment, or extra work you caused is appropriate and may reduce the severity of the punishment. Also encourage them to take responsibility or to accept the consequences.

The first response may be to dispute the punishment, especially if it seems unfair.

However taking responsibility for their own actions is a sign of maturity.

Tell them the best option may simply be to work at regaining parents' confidence.

By following the guidelines above, children will learn to control their emotions, they will learn to communicate well, they will try to see and understand their parents' point of view, which is trying to help children become better people, they will learn to build parents' confidence in them and they will also become realistic in their expectations.

Chapter Eleven
What Inheritance Is Good For The Future Of Your Children?

It is every parent's dream to work hard for his or her children.

Many parents do their best to give their children a good start in life.

Some set aside money for the children's future use.

Others make sure that their children get adequate education and learn skills that will be useful in future.

Some make sure they buy apartments or open a business for their children.

Although most parents view such gifts as legacy of love, making such provisions often puts parents under pressure to live up to the expectations of relatives, friends and the community in which they live.

Therefore, concerned parents often ask themselves, 'How much do we owe our children?'

It is only natural for parents to make provisions for their children.

Providing parental care is a serious obligation.

Certainly any parents failing to provide for those who are their own, and especially for those who are members of their household, are not fulfilling their responsibility as parents.

Granted, an inheritance is of some value, but wisdom is of much greater value than material possessions.

Wisdom, along with an inheritance, is good and is advantageous.

For wisdom is for protection, the same as money is for protection; but the advantage of knowledge is that, wisdom itself preserves alive its owners.

While money provides a measure of protection, enabling its possessor to get what he needs, it can still be lost.

On the other hand, wisdom gives the ability to use knowledge in solving problems or in attaining certain goals.

It can also safeguard a person from taking foolish risks.

Sometimes you may feel so overwhelmed by problems that you feel as though you are drowning in a whirlpool; you can imagine how much suffering could result if you made a mistake in coping with one or more of those problems!

No one is born with the ability to solve every problem successfully, making good decisions all the times. And this is where education comes in.

Where can you get education to prepare yourself to cope with life's problems?

Many, both young and old, extol the importance of an academic education. Some people even believe that it is impossible to find a decent job without a degree.

Yet there are several human needs that go beyond material achievements.

For instance, does higher learning help you to be a good parent, mate, friend or neighbour?

For that matter, people who admired for their

intellectual achievements may develop undesirable personality traits, fail in their family life, or even end up committing suicide.

Therefore the best inheritance for the children in order to make life a success includes education, which affects mind and heart, so as to transform them from within.

For example

(1) Educating them on how to be faithful to one another.

(2) Encouraging them to keep the heart clean. Without bad thoughts which may lead to bad acts which may offend and hurt others, making the mind over involves motivating it in a different direction by filling it with the best principles and instruction given by parents.

(3) Teaching them to be more patient and not to indulge in fits of anger, etc.

These are kinds of education that can free a child from vices and an immoral lifestyle.

As a result of better education, children will learn to live a better life.

By being honest and industrious, they will be appreciated by their employers.

They will become good neighbours and friends, taking an interest in the well being of their fellow man.

They will be determined to avoid vices and fleshly tendencies, so they take better care of their own health, physically, mentally, and emotionally.

Instead of wasting their resources on vices, they use them for their own good and for the good of their family.

Parents can exercise such wisdom by setting proper priorities for themselves and their children.

Material things accumulated for use by the children should not take priority over other important matters.

Printed in the United Kingdom
by Lightning Source UK Ltd.
126536UK00001B/21/A